World Building

From the Inside Out

By Janeen Ippolito

Table of Contents

Dedication

To Marilyn Montlick

the best HobbitMom a girl could have.

You taught me to take speculative fiction seriously

but not too seriously.

Introduction

World Building From the Inside Out began because of a mistake.

My mistake.

I'd been world building for over ten years. I'd studied cultures and anthropology at a college known (and infamous) for its thorough humanities program. I'd taught classes on world building and coached people through the process individually.

And yet, when it came to incorporating world building into my own speculative novels, I failed.

Over and over again.

My worlds were well designed. My races looked cool and had neat clothing and weaponry. And the names! Oh yes, I loved making up all those crazy names.

But I had missed one key factor that I should have remembered from my very first literature class: a story is about plot and characters, working towards a goal, and having disasters thrown at them. It's about excitement. Adventure. Emotional depth. Pacing.

I had beautifully-formed races with no heart. No soul. No motivation.

No reason to go along with my plot other than *because I said so*.

For some reason, that made for some pretty shallow cultures!

To use a favorite expression from my college days, I was missing the **cultural worldview**.

Worldview, the essential collection of beliefs that frame how an individual and a society perceives, interacts with, and makes decisions about the world.

Once I stopped banging my head on my desk, I did what any self-respecting, hyper-planning teacher would do: I began writing a curriculum for myself. I researched all sorts of different ideas on world building and tried out character builder profiles with pages and pages of questions.

I sifted my way through cultures and societies and compiled a set of tools to build a story culture from the worldview, instead building the geography, races, and other physical aspects and then throwing in the philosophy and beliefs as an after-thought.

The result is *World Building From the Inside Out*, a quick primer to get you to the core of your story world's cultures.

We start off with religion/philosophy. What are the essential moral and philosophical beliefs of your culture? By deciding what motivates them on a basic level, you can then figure out how your main character interacts with them, and how they in turn are products of that culture. Furthermore, it will be easier to create and manipulate conflicts between different races because you will understand their core needs and desires.

From there, we move on to government. Government is often closely entwined with religion/philosophy, and sometimes it even acts as a replacement for a religious system. After government comes society, including family structure, marital traditions, and gender roles.

For the fun of it, we touch on art, technology, naming, and food. These are often the places where you can have the most creativity.

Next come appearance and location. These categories are often the easiest to change according to what the plot requires. They are also the easiest areas to get lost in minutiae that will do nothing to further your actual plot and get that story on paper.

We end with appendices on health and medicine, military, and education. While these areas aren't strictly necessary, they can have great relevance to your personal story.

So if you're the kind of person who wants to go deep and build worlds with cultures that can integrate effectively into your plot, then this is the book for you.

Please join me on an exciting journey into the heart of man.

Or elf.

Or half-unicorn.

Or whatever else your brain can come up with!

Chapter 1 – Religion

The dreaded "R" word.

This can be a tough area to tackle for any author. Some keep religion out of their novels entirely because of possible controversy or fear of stepping on the toes of readers. However, culture is shaped around belief and worldview, and everybody believes in something. Figuring out the central beliefs of your culture is vital to understanding their core motivations.

One route is to make a religion from scratch, pulling together different existing cultural elements. J. R. R. Tolkien chose this route in *The Lord of the Rings*. The origin of Arda (the world of Middle Earth) is a mish-mash of a bunch of different mythologies, featuring a high god, Illuvatar, served by a pantheon of godlike helpers, the Valar, each with their own special part in governing Arda. Although this is a pagan concept, he threaded through elements of Christian faith with the selfish perversion of Melkor into darkness, his temptation of the elves to rebel against the Valar (and so Illuvatar) and the Marring of Arda with the destruction of the Two Trees. All of these events echo the biblical Fall of Man.

Other authors solve this dilemma by basing a religion solely on the real-life religion or philosophy they adhere to. For instance, Sharon Hinck created a quasi-Christian religion for *The Restorer*. If that's what you feel comfortable with and it works with your story, go ahead. This method also simplifies things and helps reader comprehension.

For some extra fun, show multiple belief systems. Remember that in every religion there are radical, devout, moderate, and nominal believers. Even if you decide to have one religion be the Only True

Way, it adds depth to show the different layers of belief within that religion, and within any religions which have opposing viewpoints.

Below are common forms of belief with examples and uses. This list is by no means exhaustive but should get you started.

Pantheism: equates god with the forces and laws of the universe, the idea being that god or the god-forces are in everything. Could also be the worship of all gods of different creeds, cults, or peoples indifferently, or the toleration of worship of all gods.

> *Examples:* Some examples include the Roman Empire and some sects of Hinduism. Also, the current push in the United States towards absolute toleration could be seen as a push towards pantheism.
>
> *Use:* Pantheism can be used by leadership to appease the populace and build national unity among disparate religious sects. However, this can backfire if the sects refuse to play along.

Monotheism: the belief that there is only one god. All other gods are false.

> *Examples:* Christianity. Judaism. Islam.
>
> *Use:* Monotheism is very helpful in uniting a nation towards a common purpose. Enforcing a monotheistic national religion can also help establish dictatorial rule, or even a theocracy. The more a culture associates a religion with their national identity, the more likely they are to be loyal to that nation and the function of practicing the religion will reinforce national ties. By the same token, there are always the dissenters who want a separation of church and state, which can lead to either disaffected belief in the 'national religion' or outright rebellion.

Polytheism: the belief in more than one god. This religion can overlap with animism.

> *Examples:* Greek Mythology. Roman Mythology.

Egyptian Mythology. Lots of animist religious beliefs. Note that polytheism can also include the concept of a high god who rules over lesser gods. This is different than angels, who are direct messengers of God with no power of their own except what is specifically granted to serve Him.

>*Use:* Polytheism can provide many different deities for a government to blame if things go poorly. However, can also cause conflict if one deity is perceived to favor one city-state over another (as in Greek mythology). It can be a workable system if combined with pantheism, allowing for toleration of all gods and religions. Just note that issues will come up because people will inevitably favor one god over another. Plus, there are always those pesky monotheists!

Nationalism: being loyal to and proud of your country. It often comes with the belief that your country is better than other countries. Nationalism can coexist with other religions, but can also stand alone, especially if the populace identifies with Deism or atheism as a whole. Something has to fill that religious hole in the heart, and country-worship can do the job.

>*Example:* Communist countries often fall into this category, particular North Korea. Also, the intermingling of religion with government can cause the observance of a certain religion to take on nationalist leanings.

>*Use:* Nationalism is incredibly useful in unifying a country. Countries who suppress other religions in favor of nationalism can often move very quickly in conquest and can also enforce the government ideals easily. The most extreme example is Nazi Germany (besides being an insult, Nazi does stand for National Socialist Party). The flaws in nationalism are that it can raise dissent and rebellion from citizens who feel that their individual rights are being threatened.

Deism: the belief that some kind of authority or higher power does exist, but this higher power is unknowable, or can only be known through rational observation of the physical world. Religious texts are generally considered insufficient for studying the higher power but can be adhered to as the person wishes for their personal edification.

> *Example:* The Enlightenment scholars were often Deists. Deism was a backlash against the Puritans and was a common philosophy among many of the founders of America. In addition, Deism is an undeclared belief of many nominal believers of various religions.

> *Use:* Deism is common if the culture is moving towards a science-based morality but is trying to cope with and appease those who cling to old religious traditions. Deism meshes best when the emphasis is on building a bridge between hardline scientists and hardline spiritualists.

Atheism: the belief that there is no god. This can be an active state of rebellion, a passive disinterest, or a passionate pursuit of individual reason and self-actualization. Note that something has to replace this void in the life of individuals and society as a whole.

> **Example:** Atheism includes humanist philosophies such as the Objectivist beliefs of Ayn Rand (starting with the concept that humans are born good). Atheism can also include anti-theists, such as the late Christopher Hitchens, who were dedicated to disproving the existence of God.

> **Use:** Atheism can be the natural end of a society that is burned out on trying to meld different religions together, or else has had a negative experience with religion in the past. In addition, it is quite compatible with societies that want to establish totalitarian control, and capitalist, free market societies that don't want to deal with troublesome religious censorship and morals.

Scientism: the significant trust in scientific rationalism as applied to all areas of life, from philosophy, to social sciences, to literature and art. This can possibly be the next step after a culture becomes deist or atheist.

8

Example: Vulcans in Star Trek and the Federation in Star Trek: The Next Generation, for although other religious beliefs are tolerated, ultimately science and rational thought are seen as the key to real understanding.

Use: Scientism is similar to atheism in some respects. In fact, atheism and scientism are highly compatible within the same society, although not mutually exclusive. Scientism is a more extreme view, however, and can lead to more social issues if left unchecked, as the brutality of pure observation and purely rational thought can leave little room for human compassion and grace. Scientism is thus seen in many dystopian novels.

Agnosticism: a belief of uncertainty in whether a god or high power exists or not. Agnosticism can also apply to anyone who has a doubt about any sort of religion and so doesn't want to commit. Note that some people can live normal lives without this agnostic uncertainty appearing to bother them. Others can be actively pursuing the great mystery of religious certainty.

Example: Any and all nominal believers of any religion who sporadically attend major festivals or times of worship just because of cultural tradition or "just in case." Another idea is the concept of doing good things to go to a good place, which reflects the uncertainty principle at work. If there is an afterlife, doing good things will take you there. If there isn't one, then at least it's helping someone now.

Use: Agnosticism is generally not as useful as other religions but is more of a byproduct. Anywhere there are strongly established beliefs or patterns of behavior, there will be those who are noncommittal to the cause, or else actively questioning it. Agnosticism can often be the springboard for individual characters having a conversion experience and either becoming a devout believer or an active atheist.

Animism: attributing consciousness or spiritual existence to animals or animate objects such as trees, rivers, and streams.

Animism has strong tie-ins with nature worship practices, as well as the concept of pantheism.

> ***Examples:*** When you think of animism, think of the song "The Colors of the Wind" from Disney's Pocahontas. Spirits in stones and that kind of thing. Aspects of animism are found in many tribal religions across the globe. They can also have some overlap with polytheism and the concept of ancestor worship (with the ancestors inhabiting inanimate objects).

> ***Use:*** Animism is often a trademark of tribal societies and is a way for the tribe to explain the issues of life, death, and the afterlife. It's often replaced by more complex religious systems. However, within advanced societies there can be a sense of nostalgia and purity towards the old ways, signifying a return to animist roots. Animism can either serve as a placebo for a discontented populace, or as a foundation or an uprising against the impersonal distance of modern society.

Chapter 2 – Government

Government. To some the savior of civilization. To others a dirty word. By all counts, a necessary part of world building. The kind of government you choose will directly affect how your culture will behave, and so after religion, government is the next important building block.

The idea of making a government can seem intimidating. Search engines offer you a bewildering array of choices and policies, and of course there are endless ways of making things endlessly complex.

Ignore all of that.

Remember, you're not building a massive infrastructure. You are building only what you need to help your plot make sense, and like with religion, you should feel free to modify according to your individual story. You can always make up more things later as required.

One other thing to remember is that your imagination is the limit. Forget about the real-life constraints and belief systems. Unless you're making this book a platform to push your own political agenda, leave your existing ideologies at the door. This isn't about you. This is about writing a good story.

Here are some basic questions to ask with regards to religion and government:

-How does your religion interact with your government?
-Do they support each other? Are they against each other?

-Is there separation of church and state?
-Did the government create the religion, or vice versa?

As you're answering these questions (again, as necessary), also keep in mind the overarching goal of your plot. Will the government help or hinder those goals?

One thing I want to challenge you on is try something different. It can be really easy to find yourself falling into stereotypes. Medieval or primitive setting? People often go for a monarchy. Futuristic? People often try something repressive, such as Communism.

But dare to think outside the box. How about Communism in a quasi-medieval setting? Maria V. Snyder did it in *Poison Study*, to excellent effect.

Futuristic? Why not a theocracy? Maybe one involving a pantheon of gods, like *Battlestar Galactica*'s reuse of Greek mythology.

Or what about a peaceful anarchy? A post-government society that doesn't involve violence or retribution. H.G. Wells tried it in *The Time Machine* with the Eloi. Granted, they had a rather unsavory relationship with the Morlocks, but still, it's a different perspective.

Below are key types of government. Some are based more on the way government is established, while others focus on how government is limited.

Capitalism: property is owned by individual people and companies, not by the government. Other key aspects of capitalism are the idea of free market systems without government regulation, and the idea of enlightened self-interest. Companies want to make money and grow, and so they'll invest in new opportunities and people who can help them make more money--and thus those people benefit and everybody wins.

> ***Examples:*** Two examples of capitalism are found in the United States and South Korea. A lot of other countries have aspects that are capitalist, in order to better trade with

capitalist economies. A lot of other countries have aspects that are capitalist, in order to better trade with capitalist economies.

> *Use:* Capitalism is great if you want to limit government control. Capitalist societies are generally focused on freedom of the individual over the group and personal gains over communal sharing. If you want a host of evil corporations, or some kind of fight between them, capitalism is the way to go.

Communism: the opposite of capitalism: an economic system where goods are owned by the governing authorities and are theoretically available as needed to the public. Individual rights are mostly abolished and religion is either banned or strictly controlled. Communism is meant to be the ultimate equalizer, as there is no benefit to cutthroat business deals or cheating. Everyone gets the same allotment regardless.

> *Examples:* China. Laos. Vietnam. Cuba. It is becoming increasingly difficult for Communist countries to stay Communist, as the global economy and corporate superpowers use their monetary leverage to do away with the heavy regulations. This creates a push-pull battle between the corporate empires and the Communist systems.

> *Use:* Communist ideas are the go-to economic system for dictatorships. The idea of the government owning everything creates obvious, juicy problems to mine the dark depths of the depraved soul and all kinds of opportunities for favoritism disguised as equality.

Anarchy: absence of government or any sort of established centralized authority. This can often lead to political disorder and mayhem.

> *Examples:* any country post-revolution that doesn't establish a new government system. Some post-apocalyptic situations can be found in Cormac McCarthy's *The Road*, the movie *The Book of Eli*, and the Kevin

Costner movie *The Postman*.

Use: Anarchies are often seen as gang-infested, dangerous places to be. 'Might makes right' dominates, guns and weapons are hoarded like gold (along with wet wipes and other modern conveniences), and everything revolves around survival. However, anarchy could be considered a desirable state, because it emphasizes the autonomy of individual communities, as opposed to a strong centralized government.

Republic: a type of government with elected representatives and an elected leader, instead of a king or queen.

Examples: The Old Republic in *Star Wars*. The Roman Republic. Parts of the United States government are based on the idea of a republic, although officially it's more of a representational democracy. Basically, if you see officials being elected by citizens and arguing for their constituents in a big, fancy room while another governing authority presides over the debate, you've got the makings of a republic.

Use: Republics are the model of the stable, intellectual regime. The idea of the people's wills being reflected within the highest government systems tends to inspire loyalty and a faith in the country as a whole. However, republics can have a dark side, particularly when they get too big. As in the Old Republic in *Star Wars*, in large republics unity becomes segmented and whole planets start falling through the cracks (or counties, or provinces, or what you will). Also, if republics get too big, they can move very slowly, and have difficulty responding to urgent issues.

Monarchy: traditionally, a system with a ruler who inherits their power from a family lineage. They rule for life, unless they're overthrown (or abdicate), and their governing powers range from absolute power to being a figurehead and relic of a bygone era.

Examples: In fiction, there's quite a variety to choose

14

from, as monarchies tend to be very popular. J.R.R. Tolkien does a good job outlining basic high fantasy monarchies in some of his *History of Middle Earth* books. Real life examples run the gamut between the Middle Eastern monarchies, which are basically a variety of dictatorship, to the figurehead status of English and Japanese monarchs.

Use: monarchies are quite commonly used in speculative fiction, especially high fantasy and urban fantasy. After all, what's more classic than a corrupt, false king and a wayward lost heir who is destined to take over the throne and set all things right? It's a cliché. To freshen it up, what about a ruling pair made up of a brother and sister (without the incest). Or perhaps the king is true and the upstart "lost heir" is a false little punk trying to usurp power by playing on the people's discontent?

Theocracy: government run by religious leaders who are believed to be divinely inspired by a deity or deities. Leaders might be following a sacred order left by a previously empowered person or be an empowered/prophetic person themselves. There might also be people beneath the religious leaders who run more pragmatic matters of society and infrastructure.

Examples: The Israelites in the biblical Old Testament were a theocracy, until they received and appointed King Saul. Note that while Israel was a theocracy, there were judges and other lesser leaders to handle the day-to-day duties. Islamic states such as Iran and Saudi Arabia could also be considered theocracies, as could Buddhist-dominated countries. However, theocracies are increasingly less popular in modern day societies.

Use: A theocracy can be a very effective use of control, particularly if the religion is evangelical. In this way, the country's desire to draw new members to their deity can also be a practical way of drawing in fresh population and ideas. There is also a powerful sense of unity and moral force among the people that can be a very effective tool. However, theocracies can be closed off towards other religions, to the point of violence. Education is also sometimes seen as a threat to a theocracy, with the fear that it could turn people away from spiritual matters to secular ones. A limitation on education can lead to uprisings.

Democracy: governance by the people. One person + one vote = elected leader. More complicated procedures can be layered into this formula, as well as restrictions about who can and cannot vote, and how much effect that vote can have on laws and governance.

> *Examples:* Ancient Greek city-states, most notably Athens. However, there are very few forms of modern direct democracy, where the votes of the population have direct impact on referendums and leaders. Instead, many modern governments have mixed democracy with the representational aspects of a republic, forming a democratic republic where people elect representatives to advocate for their interests in government.

> *Use:* Democracies aren't often found in fantasy, as people tend to favor the romantic ideas of kings and queens. They are seen in science fiction and urban fantasy, especially as ancient races mix with and adapt to human customs. Democracy is a great element to mix and match with other government or economic systems to create original concepts.

Dictatorship: a system where absolute power is held by a single individual or a select group of individuals. Along with this, power is handed out to lesser authorities based upon favoritism and a willingness to support the leader, and any resistance is handled with harsh penalties or death.

> *Examples:* Dictators can disguise themselves under other titles such as "Party Leader" or "President," but their strict, authoritative form of government is a dead giveaway to their true nature. North Korea and Myanmar are current dictatorships.

> *Use:* Dictatorships are go-to government systems for bad

guys. Often the evil kings or dark lords are dictators, as are the leaders of corrupt planetary or interstellar governments, such as the evil Emperor in *Star Wars*. But a creative motivation for the dictator could be a desperate, misguided need to protect their people or a personal history that leaves the leaders incapable of sharing power.

Chapter 3 – Societal Structure

Blood is thicker than water.

Religions and philosophies often hold the core beliefs of a culture, and a government binds them together, but it is the people themselves that make those concepts flesh and blood (whatever color that blood might be). They embody what it is to be a alien or a vampire or a dryad.

When you're creating a societal structure, go back to your plot. What do you need to make your good cultures good and your bad cultures bad? Does your main character align with their cultural mores, or rebel against them? What about other characters?

At the same time, don't be afraid to let your societal structure add depth and richness to your plot. Play around with customs and traditions you might need. Need a tragedy? How about throwing in the death of a loved one? For that, you'll need death rituals. Planning on an intercultural romance? Then you'll need to figure out the courtship and marital traditions of each culture so you know how they'll complement and clash with each other.

Something I want to caution you on is making your race too different and too abstractly unique. You want the audience to relate to your characters, to find them compelling and trustworthy. The less human you make them, the less prone to human trials and issues, the harder it will be to build that bond with the reader. I'm not saying it's impossible, but it's a real challenge and not one you should take up lightly.

Because societal structure is so tightly intertwined with other aspects of a culture, it's difficult to pull out options from existing types. Here's a list of choices and questions to ask yourself as you figure out your society.

Gender Roles - An important question to ask with regards to society. Is your society patriarchal, where men dominate leadership roles? Matriarchal, where females dominate leadership roles? Gender neutral, and entirely based on merit or family or class? Which gender is seen as weaker, and which as stronger? Physiology can factor into this. Which gender is responsible for earning income? For raising children? Now, the last two questions have quite a bit to do with family structure, but even so, the gender roles you decide upon will have a profound impact on how your society is shaped

Family Structure - All societies have some idea of a typical family unit. Even in the United States, which is touting an "anything goes, all is tolerated" philosophy, the societal push is towards having one or two children. More than three children can be seen as having a strong religious compulsion or a lack of access to proper birth control.

Family Structure Possibilities:
1.) community-based, with the concept of "it takes a village to raise a child"
2.) multigenerational households, with the elderly caring for the children
3.) classic nuclear family, with the essential unit being parents and children
4.) home-sharing, with two or more family units sharing the same household and responsibilities
5.) cohort living, with children living in groups by their age and being cared for by any of their parents, depending on who is assigned to which task
6.) government-raised, with children sent to state-sponsored boarding schools to be educated according to civic morals and principles

Coming of Age - What makes a boy into a man? A girl into a woman? What age does this happen? South African tribal customs involve boys 'going into the bush' to fulfill rituals and return as men. Rites of passage can involve killing something significant, eating something significant, sleeping somewhere significant, getting significant body markings, or taking significant mind-altering substances. For a girl, often the first menstrual cycle marks her ascension into womanhood, and can involve a celebration, a confinement, or in some clans, mutilation. Girls might also take part in beautification traditions and receive body marks or a clothing upgrade to indicate their new status in their community.

Courtship/Marriage Rituals - Once a child has become an adult, it's time for them to get hitched and start increasing the population! The question is, how does that happen? What are the expectations for a married couple? Is marriage considered sexual intercourse? Mental agreement? Some kind of empathic/emotional connection? If you're not writing a novel with any romance, this may not seem important. However, courtship rituals often don't have much to do with actual romance, and even include such things as arranged marriages.

Procreation - If your race is human or basically humanoid, this is fairly straightforward, and you likely learned the mechanics during a health class or in an awkward discussion with your parents. If your race is farther removed from humanoid, then you might want to consider just how different they are. Do men carry the children? Some sort of 'third gender' species? Are they made in test tubes? Again, the farther you get from the norm, the more difficult it will be for readers to identify with them. No matter what your route, there are a lot of social issues associated with procreation, and those are rich to mine for minor conflicts to add color and opportunities for conflict in your culture.

Aging Traditions - Everyone ages. Even if the race is immortal, there will often be some sense of progression from youth to maturity, regardless if there is physical decay or not. How a culture treats those who are more mature can add much-needed tension to a scenario. According to the idea of the Hero's Journey, an essential part of a main character's journey is a mentor figure, someone older who guides the young, inexperienced hero on their quest. But does your race have mentor figures? Or are the old considered weak, frail, and useless?

Death Rituals - Unless your race is absolutely immortal, death will come for them sooner or later, whether by old age, an accident, or some kind of purposeful extinction. Death is a part of life, and something that you need to consider in terms of how it affects your plot and characters actions. The right death at the right time can shift an entire plot into wonderful poignancy. The wrong death at the wrong time can cheapen scenes, throw off the mood, and alienate readers.

Chapter 4 – Art/Media

Art is all around us and is a great addition to cultural world building.

Not high art: the old paintings and statues and sculptures you see in museums. If you feel the need to create a full art history for your culture for whatever plot-related reasons, then go right ahead! But generally, that stuff is in museums, and if it's in museums, then it doesn't have as much potential to affect the culture.

What tends to affect culture more is low art: art made for monetary or business purposes, and not for the sake of art itself. In our modern-day culture, low art includes advertisements: billboards, commercials, and the ads plastered all over the side columns in your web browser window. Low art is more likely to both reflect the cultural attitudes towards beauty and the good life, and also work to alter and manipulate those viewpoints.

A major aspect of art is literature. Right away, you need to decide whether or not your culture is oral or literate. From there, think about what is relayed in those mediums. Is it more important to retain knowledge of old histories, or stay current with the daily news? If your culture has an oral tradition, is the ability to memorize and recite limited to a specialty position, or can everyone do it? If your culture has a literary tradition, can everyone read?

Low art is one of those squishy things that ties together other elements of your culture. Religion can have a lot of sway in the kind of art created, and what it is used for. Government and economic policies shape how the message is censored or not censored. Society can easily be reflected in the message or purpose behind images. Figuring out religion, government, and society is key to making decisions about art.

Here are some key aspects to consider when figuring out the place of art and media in your culture:

Concept of Beauty - What does your culture consider beautiful for men and women? Common attributes include facial symmetry, a v-shaped torso or strong muscles (man), and generous hips or pale skin (woman). If physical appearance plays little to no role in measuring others, you'll need to explain why, because that is a radical difference in a culture.

Utilitarian or Aesthetic - Every culture has priorities. Some prefer things to be aesthetically pleasing, while others favor efficient designs. A culture that values utilitarian principles to an extreme may not even have a place in society for art, music, or theater--or they may use them in very specific, concentrated ways to specifically fulfil psychological needs with minimal effort. A culture that values aesthetic principles to an extreme may prize such abilities so much that the most talented have major roles in government and politics—regardless of their actual skill in political areas.

Social Roles - The social roles of people who have art or media talent depends on the focus on the culture and the use of the media. Aesthetically-inclined cultures are more likely to encourage and promote the arts and beauty, and reward individuals in those fields accordingly. Utilitarian cultures are more likely to undervalue the arts unless they have proven usefulness. Even then, pay for art is likely to be less. Also, certain artistic areas might be dominated by certain genders. For instance, for many years in England acting was the purview of men, and skills such as weaving and embroidery the purview of women.

Customs - Societal customs such as coming of age, marriage, and death often have certain artistic elements associated with them. For instance, in Western societies, Mendelssohn's "The Wedding March" is considered a staple of many wedding ceremonies. At open-casket funerals, the body of the deceased is often made to look more lifelike by makeup and clothing, as if they are only sleeping. Media also comes into play when you consider how public or private social customs are expected to be. In previous years, putting announcements in the local newspaper was considering culturally appropriate. Now, social media is the way to made milestones official.

Specialization or Generalization - Two hundred years ago in Western cultures, the ability to sketch nature and appreciate music were considered marks of high education and class. These skills were a specialization of the elite. Nowadays, people can sign up to take art classes at local community centers or studios. Many public schools feature the basics of art in their curriculums. This shows the generalization of art into something that the populace can explore at their choice. Furthermore, there is little distinction making one type of art better than another. Specialization of art can be an excellent way to enhance the concept of a stratified society, whereas generalization of art can indicate a culture that appreciates aesthetics--or one that devalues them and believes that anyone can make good art.

Marketing - Marketing is an area where all of the other categories of this chapter tie into a larger whole. Art can be used by the government to create propaganda to promote popular initiatives or encourage support in a war. Businesses use commercials and other forms of advertisement to entice people to buy their products or services. Consider how important a good book cover is in selling a book. Concept of beauty will shape how that marketing is targeted. However, feel free to challenge this entire concept. If the culture is utilitarian, is art considered persuasive at all?

Chapter 5 – Technology

When referencing technology, it's easy to jump right to thinking about computers, cell phones, and cars. However, technology can be much simpler than that. It's merely any sort of tool that is used to make life easier and more efficient. Even a crude bear trap or a piece of bark-paper is a type of technology.

The technology we use, uses us—affects how we think and feel and make decisions. For example, researchers have discovered that when students take notes with pen and paper vs. a keyboard, they remember the pen and paper notes far better. Thus, the technology is shaping and affecting students' ability to process information.

Making up technology can be a black hole of world building. It can also be a great way to add depth to characters. A character's feelings about or access to technology can alter their ability to achieve their goals. Beliefs and access can both be determined by their choice of religion and their social status.

Another aspect to consider is that tools are often made from the existing materials in the environment. This is one area where environment plays a critical role in cultural development. If a culture lives in a plains area, it's unlikely their technology will involve using a lot of wood. Similarly, a culture living next to the ocean is more likely to develop sailing ships than one set in the mountains.

A third element that can stir up technology is the use of magic or races who are empowered by more-than-human physical traits (elemental manipulation, solar manipulation, etc). Sometimes magic can exist side by side normal technology. At other times, one impedes the use of the other, as seen in Ilona Andrews' Kate Daniels series. A third way is shown in Terry Pratchett's Discworld series: magic itself is a quantifiable unit of physics and force (sort of).

This is where all of the interdependencies of World building come to the foreground, making it overwhelming to figure out what comes first. The chicken or the egg? The music player or the plowshare?

Come back to your story. It's all about the story. Take a step back and make sure you are creating on an as-needed basis for the plot.

Also, I want to caution against the random use of technology to smooth over plot holes. This can help get through the first draft, but it will create plausibility problems later on.

Rather than go into possible technological eras, here are some different types of technology to consider when exploring this part of your culture.

Communication - From smoke signals to energy bursts, there are a litany of ways to communicate. What value does communication have in your culture? How does it affect the plot? How do the communication systems work? How can they break down? Are there alternate or secret ways of communicating below the established system?

Transportation - Does your culture use native animals? What kind? Common animals, like horses, or a new species you'll create? Does your culture have the wheel? Wheels change a lot of things, but it might be fun to figure out an alternative. The greater the level of transportation, the more likelihood for interaction with other cultures. There's also the greater chance for conquest, if that's your angle.

Writing Systems - Writing systems connect with a lot of things, including entertainment, education, communication, and record keeping/history. Has your culture invented paper? Is it even possible, using environmental resources, *to* invent paper? If not, go beyond and think of what other things your culture could use. Stone carvings? Crystal? Tattoos? If they don't have any sort of writing system, that will also impact their culture as a whole and lend to an oral system.

Note: for more details on how to use writing systems, see **Appendix 3 - Education**

Weaponry/Military - This is an area where technology can play a key role. If it doesn't, the combatants are reduced to pure hand to hand combat or magic (although if the magic involves tools, I factor it under technology). Many wars are won based on technology working or not working. Since warfare can be a common source of conflict, feel free to mix this one up. A refreshing change is to throw two very different kinds of tech at each other (Scott Westerveld does this wonderfully in his *Leviathan* series with biotechnology vs. industrial technology).

Note: for more details on Weaponry/Military, see **Appendix 2 - Military**

Entertainment/Recreation - Entertainment technology doesn't have to be television or radio. A bat and a ball are technology. A board game is technology. Often entertainment technology involves using leftover bits of tech. One example of this is horseshoes. If your character comes from a poor culture, what bits of leftover tech might they turn into a game? If they come from a rich culture, what kind of toys might they buy? Sometimes entertainment or recreation involves making technology, such as carpentry or other hands-on activities. Entertainment and recreation are staples of any culture, so if you choose to overlook this, there had better be a reason why.

Biotechnology - This involves anything from farming equipment to food preparation appliances. One of the most basic tools is a knife, scythe or other basic sharp implement to harvest food. If animals are domesticated, then plows can come into the picture. If there's some form of portable energy, then perhaps a form of tractor. In terms of food preparation, your culture can use something as simple as a leaf sewn into a bowl, to a clay pot, to blenders, food processors, or food energy replicators. Generally, biotechnology doesn't feature prominently in fiction, because sitting down and eating isn't quite as active as readers would prefer. However, if it's important to the plot, go ahead and create!

Computing - Depending the level of technology in your culture, this might not play much of a role at all. However, the basics of computing are merely the processing and calculating of information, so even a pencil and piece of paper to perform mathematical or logical equations counts. Or think of the abacus, which is still used in parts of the world. Like biotechnology, computing is an area that will either require a lot of thought, or one that can be easily skipped over.

Medicine - This is a fun aspect of culture, because often in cultures the traditional herbal remedies and physical therapies exist side by side with the more institutionalized, scientific methods of healing. Is one form culturally preferred over the other? Is one more effective than the other? Is the method the culture prefers the effective one, or is it just marketed better? Which does your character prefer? Throw a wrench in there if you want and have a third option be magical healing.

Note: for more detail on Medicine, see **Appendix 1 - Health & Medicine**

Energy - If your culture has reached the stage of power generation, how is it done? Through harnessing kinetic energy (water wheels, hand cranks)? Thermal (heat) energy? Or have they discovered electricity? Can they *make* electricity? What about nuclear power? This is also an area where magic can be featured, if you choose to use it. What are the pros and cons of using this kind of energy? Is it common, or only for the elites or the experimental?

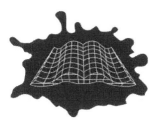

Chapter 6 – Naming

I don't have a section on languages for a simple reason: it can be a bottomless pit of distraction from writing your story.

Don't get me wrong. Word and language creation can be one of the joys of world building. However, they can also be one of the biggest black holes standing in the way of writers completing their goals.

"Wait," you might argue, "wasn't the great J. R. R. Tolkien inspired by the creation of his languages Quenya and Sindarin to write the classic *The Lord of the Rings*?"

True. But here are some other details about Tolkien:

1.) He was a professor with a deep interest in philology (historical linguistics/literary criticism).
2.) He never finished Quenya or Sindarin.
3.) His busy schedule (and the tiny event known as World War II) meant that *The Lord of the Rings* wasn't finished until twelve years after he started it.

History lesson over. The point is, we all have busy schedules, and writing time is at a premium. If you want to go ahead and create an in-depth language (or languages) for your story world, far be it from me to stop you.

But the goal of this primer is to help you build a culture so you can keep writing your story.

So let's move to an inherently useful part of linguistic world building. Names. Because your story has nouns: people, places,

29

things, and ideas. Nouns need awesome names.

Sometimes names are intuitively easy. Characters come right to you, full of themselves and ready with a name. At other times, those characters end up dubbed MC (main character) or BB (Big Bad) for half the draft. The same thing can be true for locations and the names of specific objects.

Consider the following when you're in need of new names:

Characters - Protagonist and antagonist are key, of course, as are significant supporting characters. Beware of over-indulging in naming every single minor character something Significant.

Places - Only focus on naming key areas in your story. These could be countries, continents, geographical features such as mountains, or constructed locations, such as palaces. Often in stories, people stick with simple names: Iron Hills, White Plains, Crystal Caves. This is a safe choice and is true to life. Consider that the home of the president of the United States is called "The White House" and *is* a white house. However, feel free to switch things up by having a few quirky names that reflect an important historical event, or places that are named after an important figure.

Objects - These named objects could be significant amulets, epic space vessels, or other special items. They could also be items unique to your world or land that aren't common to Earth. Make sure to include description with foreign objects so that the reader can picture them, but don't fall prey to the need to rename everything—be careful to consider the context. In one of my novels, my main character wears a sweatshirt. I could call it a fleecy tunic or a layered top or a lined shirt. But this is an alternate universe urban fantasy setting, not a medieval one or a futuristic one. So I just used the word 'sweatshirt' and moved on with the story.

Ideas - Consider what concepts set your culture(s) apart from the norm. What about love? Maturity? These ideas likely need their own unique word. For instance, the Greek language has at least four main words for love, depending on the relational context. Your priority ideas will also reveal the priorities of the culture.

Mandarin Chinese has specific words for the relatives on the paternal and maternal side, as well as their hierarchy of ages. What are the key concepts in your culture?

Usage - At their core, names mean ownership and belonging. They are a way for people of a certain group to connect to each other, whether it be through family ties, political parties, or gang membership. How do names function in your culture? How do they show relationship and ownership between people? Often this is through having a last name or being given a new name to show acceptance in a group.

Amount - This concerns how many names an individual can accumulate. In Western societies, the individual's name comes first, and the surname (family name) comes second. Sometimes a middle name is added. However, in some Asian societies, the family name comes first and the individual's name comes second. This shows a priority of family over individual.

Dubbing - Who gives the names in your culture? Often, family does so. How are those names chosen? This can be a highly idiosyncratic choice, but there are trends and traditions within cultures. One is to name a baby after a respected ancestor or important historical figure. Religious adherents in particular tend to name their children after significant figures in their belief system. Tolkien had one of his elven races allow individuals to choose their own, additional name after a certain period.

Ceremony - This concerns how an individual is named. Religion comes into play when the parents dedicate or christen their children in a public ceremony. At other times, registering a child's name with the state might be the important factor. Or none of the above could be important, especially when socioeconomic class is considered. Historically, children from rich families have had more ceremony and attention than those of poor families. What is the case in your culture?

Age - Nowadays, in many cultures, children are named as soon as they are born. However, in times past, children wouldn't be named until they had lived a certain amount of time, due to the frequency of infant mortality. Consider the health and wellness of your race.

Does this affect their naming? What about coming of age? Does naming feature into that?

Alteration - Sometimes, a rose by any other name might smell sweeter. How are names changed in your culture? Is that even possible? This is another category that depends on your individual characters, but the process and cultural attitude towards name changing can be more established. If an individual alters their name, are they considered suspect? Or is name alteration required to join (or leave) a certain religious, political, or societal group?

Terms of endearment - How is affection expressed in your culture? Words of affirmation and love are considered highly important to many. The words "sweetie," "hon," and "darling" are often heard among southern areas of the United States. However, in other regions such words are considered informal, or even demeaning. Are terms of endearment or affection acceptable in your culture? If so, in what contexts?

Insults - Insults are their own kind of naming, debasing an individual or making fun of them through calling them by new words. In some cultures, this might be considered playful or teasing, while it others, it could be as terrible as outright profanity. What is considered acceptable in your culture? Also consider that generally, among humans the female gender tends to towards veiled insults, while males tend towards more direct attacks. However, this is your world, so feel free to mix things up.

Titles - Mister and misses. Ma'am and sir. These are just a few examples of titles that are often tacked onto names. For clarity's sake, it's often easier to use these titles. However, in some cases switching up a few higher-ranking names might be just the right touch of uniqueness. For instance, instead of having a king, have a patron or a lawgiver. Just make sure your readers understand the meaning of the title.

Animals - Naming something implies relationship. A negative name towards an animal shows a lack of regard, whereas a positive name elevates the beast to a special position. A complete lack of name often reveals that there is little point to naming and is often reserved for creatures who are being hunted, raised for slaughter, or seen as irrelevant. What is your culture's attitude toward animals?

Name Litmus Test

1.) Can the reader pronounce the name? Readers will forgive a lot, and they aren't necessarily reading the book aloud–but then again, they might! Do you really want them to be processing your overly-complicated name as "blah" or some other space filler? To test this out, have a friend or two pronounce the name without any coaching from you. Is their pronunciation close to how *you* want the name pronounced?

2.) Does the name sound like any other words in the story? Make it intentional. Some readers are going to read into it anyway. You might as well work with this. Otherwise, try to switch things up. One of my downfalls is a love for names beginning in "a" or "t" or "l" - and I've had kind friends point out when too many characters have names that start with one of these letters.

3.) Is the name longer than five syllables? If so, I humbly ask that you reconsider. High fantasy epics are particularly prone to extra-long names of Significance and Meaning and Purpose. But we live in a time of brevity. The Sacred Scroll of Gysonithwiella could just as easily be Gysonith or even Gyson, and as long as the plot is good, the reader will not know the difference. An alternative is to introduce the name, and then soon after have the characters use an abbreviation or acronym.

4.) Does the name rhyme? Refer to rule two. If names rhyme, it should be intentional. Andrew Peterson did this well in his *Wingfeather* books with the "Fangs of Dang." Memorable, whimsical, and evocative. Just be aware that rhyming can come off as humorous (think Dr. Seuss).

Chapter 7 – Food

It's best to focus on writing about food the way you should eat food—in moderate amounts, just enough to fill in the nooks and crannies of your culture and add detail to your character and plot.

Whether or not it is necessary for your race to eat is up to you, particularly with regards to types of food. Certainly in the world's cultures, anything from guinea pig to pig ears is acceptable, and that doesn't even factor insects (or arachnids). Or maybe the culture survives on nutrient-laced air? Whatever they like to feast upon, there are certain things that you might need to figure out to fully flesh out the culture.

Usually, I've been referencing existing works of fiction to use as examples. However, in the case of food I urge you to simply Google search different cultures and their eating habits. There is a bounty of insight and ideas to be used with care and discretion.

Favorite Foods - These do not have to be common or easily-found foods. Favorite foods are often determined by having emotional, geographical, or even financial significance. Christmas foods are often considered favorites because of the memories they evoke of the holiday. Lobsters are often considered a favorite food in coastal New England because it's easy to get them and seafood is part of the culture. Peanuts are a favorite in the South because they are a major cash crop. What are favorites in your culture?

National Foods - What foods are considered representative of your culture? For America, a few foods are hamburgers and hotdogs and popsicles. In England, Shepherd's Pie, tea and scones, and fish and chips are considering the norm. For Japan, everyone thinks of sushi and sashimi and seafood-based delights. What foods are your culture known for? What are they stereotyped for?

Religious Foods - Go back to your religious elements. What foods are associated with different religions? Consider the Catholic tradition of eating fish on Fridays or fasting during Lent. Jewish customary foods include gefilte fish and kugel. Another area to consider is what foods are taboo. In Islam, eating pig products is forbidden. Many Hindus consider cows sacred and will not eat beef. Are there foods that religious adherents in your culture should not eat?

Taboo Foods - Apart from religion, there are other foods that cultures generally considered untouchable. In America, eating animal brains and genitals is largely considered repulsive, except in certain regional cuisines. People from other cultures often consider processed foods like canned cheese or cheese slices to be abhorrent. One way to determine taboo foods is to start from a culture's comfort foods and national foods, and work towards the opposite end. For instance, in America people generally prefer fish cooked or at least smoked. The idea of eating raw fish is considered disgusting to many.

Holiday Foods - For this, you need to figure out holidays. If holidays don't need to factor into your plot and you don't need to refer to them, then skip over this section. However, if there are holidays, then think about what food is involved. Thanksgiving involves turkey and pumpkin pie. Scottish Hogmanay wouldn't be complete without haggis (stuffed sheep stomachs). And round pastries are essential for Chinese moon festivals. What foods reflect the themes and surroundings of your holiday?

Coveted Foods - These are the foods worth a lot of money, or the foods that could be given as fancy presents. What brands or types of food are considered worth saving up for as a once a year treat? Why? Consider location. This might be something like fresh mangoes in Siberia, or venison in the Bahamas. It could also be something rare, such as truffles or expensive wines. Also, it might be demand that drives the price up. Halloween candy is in demand before the holiday, and marked down ninety percent after.

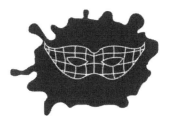

Chapter 8 – Appearance

Naturally, how you choose to make your people look is up to you. Sometimes a character's face or physical appearance will come in a flash, and then you try to build a culture around that idea. At other times, it's a long process.

Remember that your readers will have certain preconceptions about how humans tolerate various physical differences and how their clothing and appearance reflects different social environments. For instance, if someone is poor, the expectation is that their clothing is ragged and of low quality. If you decide to buck that tradition, go right ahead—but be prepared to explain why. Besides clothing, consider forms of body modification such as tattoos, piercings, and hair styles. Do these have any bearing in your culture? Why or why not?

Another factor to consider in your culture is diversity. Notice I keep saying "culture" and not "race." You could have a mono-racial culture, which is isolated from others for their own reasons (anything from religious to geographical). You could also have a multiracial culture, which is more likely societies located near major geographical thruways, or in societies that rely heavily on commerce. Either way, racism will play a factor. People are bound to treat others differently based on their appearance. If they don't, again, figure out why they don't, because this is a universal quality. How are people of mixed identities treated?

Here are categories to consider:

Location – All races usually have certain adaptations to their environment. Typical humanoids can have rougher skin and risk dehydration in a dry environment, such as a desert or an icy area.

Does your culture have special physical characteristics to resist this? Do they wear special protective clothing? In addition, hot climates will cause inhabitants to wear loose clothing, or else less clothing, whereas cold climates will lend towards layers of clothing. If this isn't the case for your culture, then explain why-- give your race some special quirk that makes them resistant to or unaffected by these outside stressors. Also, greater exposure to ultraviolet radiation (perhaps cause by more than one sun) tends to affect skin tone. If it doesn't for your race, why?

Socioeconomic Status - As I mentioned earlier, the difference between the poor and rich is one of the more obvious things to show in physical appearance. A common trope is that impoverished are less healthy, have far dirtier and worn clothing, and will appear unwashed, whereas the wealthy will be healthy, well-fed, and clean.

However, fashion plays a role in this as well. At one time, it was popular to imitate Queen Elizabeth by blacking out one's teeth, and a desire for pale faces caused people to powder themselves with dangerous chemicals. In these situations, the poor might in fact be healthier. In addition, people with certain physical traits are often relegated to lower class. Is this the case in your culture?

Occupation - In American culture, cooks tend to wear aprons, with higher status chefs often wearing all white clothing. Referees wear black and white stripes. Store clerks wear colors or uniforms associated with their company. How is this reflected in your culture? What clothing is typical for different jobs? Is there slang for these jobs based on their clothing? Are people of certain physical appearances naturally considered suited for certain jobs?

Gender Roles – It's common for cultures to have gender-specific physical differences other than reproductive organs. Very frequently, there are cultural norms for what is acceptable for males and females to wear. If your culture does not have this divide, you will need to explain or show why. Often divisions are based on concepts of modesty. What are taboo areas or body parts that must be covered up? Are these areas the same for males as they are for females?

Age - How does your culture show age? Through wrinkles and grey hair, or something else? What is customary for children to wear? Note that higher status or wealthier children will often have more rules and fashions, whereas lower status or poorer children will wear simple clothing from available resources.

Is there a time period, a coming of age, when the clothing for young men and young women changes? What about marriage? Is there a significant age when older people wear different clothing? What is burial clothing like?

Group Allegiance - In a culture, a group allegiance can be anything from gangs, to sports teams, to religious groups. Are certain colors, physical characteristics, or clothing part of certain political or social groups? What about tattoos or other markings? Consider how the Amish wear varying types of plain clothing, often shunning buttons. In addition, the married men have beards. Is there any need to show this kind of allegiance in your story?

Chapter 9 – Location

At last we reach the outermost part of our journey--the setting of the story. Setting, like all other aspects discussed in this book, needs to serve characters and story above all.

Please do not be afraid to alter your setting to suit your plot. Never depend on setting to exclusively sell your plot. While there are books that focus heavily on long descriptions, their time has passed from the general market. If you want your plot to reach and bless the most people, you need to grab their hearts with character and story first, and then fuse your awesome world building into each scene.

Yet, there is a place to focus on geography. The sky (and far beyond) is the limit for location, and there are great world building books that only focus on geography. Additionally, I'm hoping you can come up with even crazier and more original ideas from your own head! However, there are some basic choices you can make with location and culture that will help integrate them into your plot.

Urban - This involves any kind of city environment. An urban location can be a ruined cityscape of a dystopian world, a utopian steampunk edifice from the past, or an upscale futuristic paradise from a science fiction world. The most important aspect is that the city (or cities) is featured, with a life and pulse of its own. Some cultural aspects of this type of environment are a sense of comfort from the skyscrapers/walls, a faster pace and lifestyle, and a greater chance for people from different cultural backgrounds to mingle. Because of the nature of urban life, even though there are definite economic tiers, the smaller geographical location makes it possible for people from very different backgrounds to interact. This can create a lot of conflict. Plus, if chaos is unleashed, a lot of lives could be at stake, and that always increases the tension.

Rural - This cultural location involves any kind of small town or countrified environment. The most extreme version is an isolated farm, or a cabin in the woods. These areas lend a feeling of loneliness and the mystery of being close to vast amounts of forest or wildlands with their own secrets to hide. Add in a local small town, and you have social claustrophobia, formed from everyone knowing each other's names and business. This can be another great tension builder for plots, especially if the main character is a stranger coming to a new town—or a member of that town noticing a stranger. Note that the feeling of small town rural can easily transfer to a small space station or a deserted island.

Hostile - Whatever sort of environment you choose, whether or not it is hostile can play a vital role in conflict and in pushing the plot forward. Note that hostile can vary according to the physiology of your culture. A desert environment is hostile to a fish, but perfectly accommodating to many kinds of snakes and lizards. If your culture lives in a hostile environment, why? Were they forced there by conquest? Was there a horrible catastrophe? Is it a form of penance? How do they adapt to this environment?

Idyllic - Idyllic environments would seem to be difficult to use, because the environment is accommodating to the needs of the culture around it. However, it can be a great way to introduce a conflict by having another outside force threaten to turn the idyllic into the hostile. Consider how many disaster movies start off in seemingly perfect locations. Another way to introduce conflict is to have it start from the inside. There's nothing like the contrast between a beautiful location and the ugliness and awful intrigue of the people living there. For idyllic environments, there's often nowhere to go but down, and that is ripe with possibilities.

Familiar - What makes a familiar location narrows in on your protagonist's specific journey. Is their location one where they have grown up their entire life? Do they have memories ingrained with certain areas - favorite playgrounds, that old tree/pole/random plant object where they were bullied? The advantage of the location being familiar is that you can use it to reveal a lot about the character's backstory in a very external way. It also works to limit your point of view, because the character might miss things due to familiarity. Alternatively, they may notice things more, because any difference is peculiar. Introducing a new idea to a familiar location can be a great way to build mystery and tension. Just be careful to show things enough to the reader, who obviously isn't as familiar with the setting as the character is.

Foreign - This is where you place the character in the middle of foreign territory. They don't speak the language, they don't understand the culture, and they are constantly making mistakes. If they aren't, that needs to be explained right away, because making mistakes in new locations and cultures is a universal constant. This cultural and environmental bewilderment allows the reader to learn about the culture along with the protagonist, which can breed instant reader identification and sympathy. Tension is also natural, as there are plenty of ways to hide what's coming next from the ignorant main character. However, being in a foreign location can also be exhausting to read, and repetitive, as other characters have to constantly explain things to the protagonist. If you're not careful, your narrative can come across as a guidebook instead of a story.

Appendices

I'm constantly exploring cultures and coming up with new ideas. One reason I decided to publish a second edition of this book was that I had to share all this new content!

The following chapters are not strictly necessary to world building. However, you might find that they are helpful to your world. If nothing else, you'll be a little wiser and know some cool facts!

Appendix 1 – Health and Medicine

Laughter is the best medicine. Or is it? Could you really create a culture where laughter heals all ills?

Of course you can! Because this is fiction and we do things like that.

Medical care and health care are critical parts of any culture. From what is considered an illness to how the sick are treated, there are plenty of ways to expand this area of culture to allow for more growth and opportunities for tension.

Of course, if your race is humanoid and you don't want to focus on this, then go ahead and move on to the next chapter. However, consider carefully whether you want to give health and medicine a quick skim. You never know what could inspire a plot twist!

Medical help often comes in two flavors: traditional and scientific. For the fun of it, we'll also toss in magical.

Traditional deals with what a culture has historically done for health and wellness. This can include folk or herbal remedies, as well as food or drink tonics. If a medicine was passed down from generation to generation or made with a secret recipe by a great-grandma, it falls under traditional. This is also where healing techniques can overlap with religious beliefs.

Scientific deals with the advancements a culture is making in the field of medicine using the scientific method and modern technology. This typically involves labs, microscopes, pills, and technological devices. There is often a clash between traditional and scientific medical treatments, but there doesn't need to be. Finding a way to have the two intermingle would be a fresh take on the material!

Magical deals with how magic interacts with the other two systems. Usually magic is intermingled with traditional healing methods, but there are possibilities to mix it with scientific. For instance, if magic on your world is defined as a neutral energy force that can be used for good or evil, then why not use magic to power modern medical technology? If your story defines magic as purely negative, then medicinal use will be more problematic. Using magic for healing may have some nasty side effects—or magic could even be the cause of the ailment.

Here are some other areas to consider:

Chronology – In history, traditional methods often come first, followed by scientific, following a natural sense of technological progression. However, it is also possible to have a technological regression. This is common in post-apocalyptic and dystopian stories. Scientific methods are a thing of the past, perhaps even equated with magic, and traditional medicine is the only possibility. A scientific society could also choose to explore traditional methods out of nostalgia, a desire to connect with a more spiritual, natural force, or a quest to gain magical power.

Common Ailments – Our most common ailment is the common cold, with its plethora of symptoms: sneezing, coughing, aches and pains. Are the symptoms the same in your culture? Or is there another ailment that plagues the people? Make sure to consider treatment options and how this ailment is passed from person to person. You could also work this into the humor or sayings of your culture.

Superficial Ailments – Pimples. Loose skin under the chin or upper arms. Sagging breasts. Gray hair. All of these are "ailments" that people treat using basic or complicated procedures. Are they necessary? In most cases, no. However, that doesn't stop people from spending money to fix such issues. Ailments like these could be used as a way to poke fun at a character, to hint at a more serious condition, or to show the qualities of vanity or pride.

Serious Ailments – This is where you can get into plot twists. Serious ailments include things like cancer, muscular dystrophy, and other degenerative or difficult-to-cure diseases. Note that introducing diseases like this to your culture almost necessitates use in the plot, whether due to an environmental force causing the ailment or one of the supporting or main characters falling prey to the serious ailment. Be sure to do your research to make sure this twist is handled carefully, or it could spiral into melodrama.

Enhancements – These are completely unnecessary procedures that people do in pursuit of beauty. From neck lengthening to tattoos to lip plugs, enhancements are cultural ways for people to show their coming of age, beauty, masculinity, or other ideal qualities. This area you can have a lot of fun with, especially as you research the awesome things in actual world cultures. Just be respectful about borrowing a real custom and make sure it actually fits with your culture, instead of just tossing it in there for kicks.

Mental Illness – Mental illness is a rather difficult field to research in real life, much less create for a story. A lot of writers lump any form of mental illness under the category of "madness" to avoid complications; however, this overlooks a way to enrich the difficulties of characters. What kind of mental illnesses are common? Are they treated by healers or doctors, or are there specialized caretakers such as psychologists or psychiatrists? In addition to neurological conditions, some mental illness involves an unhealthy or maladaptive perspective. Therefore, you need to understand what a healthy perspective and worldview entails in your culture--and that goes back to the core worldview and beliefs.

Disabilities/Chronic Illness – These two are lumped together because they both involve issues that fundamentally alter the way an individual can participate with the normal activities of their culture. Under the category of disability and chronic illness is everything from a limp to allergies to diabetes. This can be a good category to explore for plot twists for your character. One trend in fiction is to keep the protagonists free of any disabilities or chronic conditions, because these issues get in the way of heroism. However, making the protagonist, or even supporting characters, suffer from a disability or chronic ailment can add depth, vulnerability, empathy, and diversity. Just do your research well and use as it benefits the plot.

Environmental Effects – The environment can be helpful—or dangerous. Mold is a common cause of illness and even death. On the other hand, Superman and Supergirl get their powers from being under a yellow sun. You could also make being on certain parts of land grant certain abilities and being on other sections prevents those same abilities from being used.

Habitual Rituals – Brushing teeth. Washing hair. Clipping fingernails and toenails. All of these are daily tasks that are considered normal for civilized people. It's fine to transfer those habitual activities over to your culture, especially if the culture is humanoid. However, feel free to add some individual quirks, or perhaps different devices to accomplish these same tasks. If your race isn't humanoid, think about what cleansing rituals they might require based on the differences in their physiology. For instance, a birdlike race might require daily feather preening, dust baths, or beak grinding.

Practitioners – In part, practitioners will depend on whether you choose the traditional or scientific route. Traditional medicine tends to use words like "healer" and involve apprenticeship and hands-on training. Scientific medicine follows a system of in-class instruction, higher mathematics and a clinical approach involving homework and exams. Some stories choose to combine the two methods, which can add interest. For instance, you could create a race where a medical practitioner must master traditional techniques as well as scientific exams. Or perhaps yours is a culture where *everyone* learns healing, to some degree, sort of like mandatory CPR and first aid training.

Perspectives on Illness – There are three common perspectives on what causes illness. Two perspectives align with traditional medicine: (1) supernatural forces or (2) being out of balance with the natural environment. The third perspective treats the body as a mechanical device to be fixed, and so aligns with the scientific method. If a culture adheres to the supernatural forces method, they might assume a disease or disability is a curse. A culture

47

favoring the natural environment perspective might see illness as an issue of energy forces or eating incorrect food for the season. The body-as-machine perspective will see illness as something to be treated with tested pharmaceuticals.

Preventive Measures – This involves what a culture does to prevent various ailments from occurring. Preventative measures can be anything from vaccines, taking oil of oregano, or wearing certain colors. Note that preventative measures do not have to be particularly effective to be valued in the culture, and there is often controversy over which measures are more effective. In addition, preventative measures can move from being health-based to having other socio-cultural roles. One example is the wearing of surgical masks in some Asian cultures to combat poor air quality and the spread of airborne illness. Now masks have also become a way of avoiding contact with others, similar to putting on earbuds or headphones.

Appendix 2 – Military

What is war good for?

In terms of writing, a lot. Conflicts and warfare form the core of many plots, especially in speculative fiction. While realistic fiction tends toward an in-depth study of martial systems, sometimes the speculative side gets the short end of the stick. After all, throw in enough wizards with magic or spaceships with lasers, and voila: battles!

Perhaps your story doesn't involve much in the way of battles or warfare. There are plenty of stories that can hum along just fine without this area. However, the way a culture conducts itself in the military can be quite revealing.

Here are some important factors to consider:

Purpose – Every military has a reason for existence. A conquering culture may build a military for offensive purposes or preemptive strikes. An isolationist culture may create a military to ensure their borders are impermeable to outsiders. A primarily commercial culture may be interested in protecting their business or trade interests. Or perhaps the military was a reaction to an attack from another culture. Whatever the reason, it will affect how and to what degree a military system will manifest.

Potency – Consider your military with respect to surrounding cultures. Is your culture a major military power, or are they only keeping enough of a force to protect themselves or serve as a ceremonial guard? Are they competing with another culture for the best weaponry, like the Space Race between the United States and the U.S.S.R.? Whatever the reason, bear in mind that your culture's overall potency will be determined by their advancement with respect to surrounding cultures.

Parameters – Along with potency comes parameters—the limitations of your culture's military power. Is it bound by the borders of your country? Does the military have jurisdiction within your country? In other words, can soldiers arrest civilians? Perhaps there is no distinction between civilian police and government military enforcers. Perhaps there are ten different categories. It all depends on what the plot wants and how this ties into your other established systems.

History – Every military has a reason for its creation. What was the original purpose for this military force? Has that purpose changed? If so, explain why. Also, consider how the military presence in your culture has changed over the years. Has it become more militarized? Less? Has serving in the military risen or fallen in status? Only explore as far as you need for the plot.

Military Heroes – Most cultures have military heroes. If your culture isn't the type to venerate heroes, that is a unique aspect that should be explored more in societal structure. Also, consider what kind of behavior is considered heroic. Self-sacrifice and courage in the face of imminent danger are qualities that will easily relate to readers. However, favoring different qualities can make your race more alien, if that's the angle you want.

Types of Military Branches – This is often determined by geographical factors. Most of the time it doesn't make sense for a desert country to have a navy, or an underground colony to have airships. However, this is speculative fiction, so if it works for your plot, go for it! Two other aspects that influence military branches are tradition and pragmatism. An example of tradition is where your space-faring race has an elite saber commando team, even though everyone has body armor that's thinner than cotton but resists all physical weapons and attacks. An example of pragmatism is where your underground colony is being attacked by dragons who are threatening to make the underground chambers cave in. This might be a reason to invest in airplanes or airships.

Leadership – In the United States, the president bears the title of commander in chief of the armed forces. Who is the head of your military force? Does each branch have its own leader? This is critical to know, because the leadership sets the tone for the entire military. Are leaders bureaucrats who insist on order and red tape, hard-charging commanders groomed at academies, royalty there for ceremony, or maybe a dictator who simply doesn't trust others?

Ranks – The United States military ranking system is based on the Prussian system, but until the mid-1800s the majority of global powers did not use the officer/enlisted system. What is the structure of your ranks? How does the military's chain of command work? How does this affect the day to day life of the soldier? An ordinary soldier disrupting the chain of command or storming the office of a superior officer is a great way to add tension and conflict.

Enlistment – How is your military staffed? The two main options are voluntary enrollment and involuntary conscription via a draft system. The choice here indicates a lot about the culture. If enrollment is voluntary, there are often perks to the position of soldier and society has a positive view of the activity. If conscription is the norm, the military can be seen as more of a necessary duty, and there may not be as much prestige attached to it. Some other options include being open to foreign enrollment, as is the case in the French Foreign Legion, or requiring all citizens to have military service, as is the case with Israeli citizens.

Exclusions – Every culture has individuals who are considered unsuitable for military service. In some countries, women are forbidden from direct combat scenarios. Is this true in your world? Why? Other exclusions could be based on race. Some militaries only allow native citizens to serve. Others might exclude certain kinds of criminals. Other possible exclusions can be due to physical or mental disability, the onset of disease, or religious belief.

Support Staff – These are the positions necessary to support combat soldiers. Military support staff often work on forts or bases. Are there bases within your country's borders, or within other countries? Consider transportation, medical care, maintenance of weaponry and other technology, engineering, tactical planning, food services, and even janitorial duties. Also, what role, if any, does religion have in the military? Is the service formed of only one religious sect? Is religion forbidden from being openly spoken about? Or are there services for the devout and burial rituals for them?

Duration of Service – Most militaries have a minimum length of service. This could be determined by the severity of the conflict, the physical toil of active combat, or life span of the culture. There could also be a maximum length of service. Again, life span often plays a role, at least in active combat where soldiers need to be at their peak of ability. If you've created a race that doesn't age normally, then this may affect duration as well.

Post-Military Life – Veterans can return home a hero, a villain, or in a body bag. How are they treated in your culture? Are veterans permitted to join regular society, or do they simply move into support staff once they age out of active duty? Whatever you choose, there needs to be a reason behind it. Also, is there a support system for the ex-military to lean on? Some examples of this include counseling, job skill training, college scholarships, a stipend, or room and board. And if this is available, who pays for it? Who takes care of people left permanently disabled by military action?

Popular Opinion – What is the general populace's attitude towards the military? Do they see it as a necessary evil, or a glorious duty? The answer to this question is heavily tied into how the military originated, what its primary purposes are, and its parameters. A populace is less likely to be friendly towards an invasive military system where they could be arrested at any moment. They can be friendlier towards a system that recruits loyal citizens and trains them to protect civilians against outsiders.

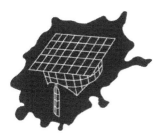

Appendix 3 – Education

Reading, writing, and 'rithmetic.

Bad example of alliteration. But good example of the main focus of American education at one time: teaching the basic principles of reading comprehension, writing, and mathematics.

Now that we are well into the Information Age, many other subjects are considered critical for students to understand, including computers, technology, and intercultural skills. This is just one example of how education adapts and changes to fit a culture.

Level of education is a standard aspect to consider in characterization. Make that character's level of education have significance (whether good or bad) within their culture and you suddenly have an additional level of connection or conflict. Figuring out the basics of education within your culture can be an easy way to add depth.

Here are some areas to consider:

Optional or Compulsory – Compulsory education indicates a high value for literacy and intelligence within the culture. Reasons for educating the general population include having an informed public to participate in civic affairs and encouraging improvement in various academic fields to surpass other countries in science or technology. A culture that makes education optional may be one that either has less centralized authority or sees an educated populace as a threat.

Restrictions – Forbidding certain individuals from education is common in many cultures. Some exclusions are based on gender, usually with females being seen as less capable of or interested in education, or race, out of a desire to keep certain races out of the country or perceiving them as a threat.

Another form of restriction includes segregation policies, where individuals are divided into different (and often unequal) schools for a supposed benefit. This is a natural consequence of gender, racial, economic, or other tensions.

Duration of Education – This is where timing comes into play. How long is a school day? A school year? How long do students have to be educated before they receive a degree or other recognition of achievement? Agricultural or lower-class communities often have less education. Urban or upper-class communities tend to place a higher priority on education, either for advanced careers or for increased social status.

Structure of Education – Structure concerns how a school day functions. In earlier times, students from poorer economic circumstances would all learn in one room, and the teacher had to be capable of teaching at all levels. This is still true in some developing countries. Many modern primary schools have one designated teacher per classroom who teaches all subjects. When the subjects become more advance in middle and/or high school, each instructor teaches a certain subject, and the students move between classes. In college, often both the instructor and the students move to different classrooms, as instructors have their own offices.

Physical Location of Education – This involves the location and layout of the actual school building. It could be under a tree, crowded on wooden benches in a single room, or individualized learning pods on a spaceship. Aspects of physical location are important because they are deliberate ways of shaping the students. This category also includes physical methods of maintaining order within a school. For instance, the use of bells to signal class changes is traced back to the industrial revolution, which trained students to respond to bells to prepare them for future factory work. Today, some schools are phasing out the use of bells because factory work is not as prevalent. When considering location, think about how the environment will mold and shape the students.

Style of Instruction – Some schools prefer tracking results, and while students participate in group work, major tests and assignments are often completed individually. This indicates an individualistic culture with emphasis on personal achievement. Another type of school prefers that students speak to each other when they have trouble with a lesson and develop interpersonal skills by solving the problem together. This preference can indicate a more cooperative culture, where the sum is seen as greater than the parts. When considering the style of instruction, remember that this important detail says a lot about what the culture values and wants to instill in its youth.

Instructor Training – In Finland, instructors must have specialized master's degrees. In the United States, public education requires a four-year teaching degree, but some private schools do not. What are the education requirements of instructors in your culture? Note that higher standards also mean that fewer teachers will qualify, which might not work in a culture dispersed over a large area Also, consider the reputation of the teaching career. Is teaching seen as a respected profession with commensurate pay, or is it seen as a service industry? This ties in closely with how much education is valued by the government and by the general populace, as well as cultural objectives.

Higher Education – Higher education might not exist in a lower-class setting, or in a culture that doesn't value intellectual achievement. Colleges and universities are a sign of a culture that has moved from agrarian to the industrial revolution and beyond. There might also be an emphasis on only certain kinds of higher education, in areas that are practical to the culture: medicine, law, engineering, or religion. .

Valued Fields – Human cultures tend to value what has everyday use. This means that certain fields of study will advance, and will be rewarded with good pay and respect in the community; other fields may attract students, but won't lead to a decent living. Jobs that commonly lead to well-paying careers in Western cultures are business, law, medicine, engineering, and the sciences. This favoritism reveals a cultural respect for economic prosperity through capitalism, legal representation, healthcare, and technology. Note that other fields such as social work, education, and journalism could be valuable *to* the culture, but are not valued as much *by* the culture in terms of reimbursement and prestige. What are the core values of your culture, and how will they manifest in education?

Funding – In some cultures, the government pays for education. In others, parents or other guardian figures are expected to pay. What is the case in your culture? If the government funds education, that shows a high value in educating the populace. Not all governments want to give this kind of empowerment, lest the civilians revolt. Government-funded education also gives the government more input on what is being taught and could turn education into a propaganda tool. Private education tends to be more expensive and can lead to a greater separation between educational haves and have-nots.

Types of Education – Below are different types of education you can explore, expand upon, twist, adapt, or otherwise alter to suit your world building needs.

> **Homeschool** - education at home by the parents and/or an organization of parents

> **Cyber-school** - education in a school system through the use of internet technology

> **Religious** - education that involves being taught subjects from a religious worldview

> **Preparatory School** - elite form of upper schooling designed to prepare students for higher education

> **Private** - education that is separate from whatever public education is available

> **Apprenticeship** - education involving a novice applying for instruction to a master in a particular field

Boarding School - education where a student leaves their family unit and is raised at the institution while attending classes

Reform School - education for students who are juvenile delinquents, intended to quell and reform bad behavior

Military School - high school preparatory schools (often boarding schools) designed with a military structure for additional discipline and to ready students for service in the military

Specialized Educational Styles - Montessori, Goddard, Classical, Charlotte Mason, Homeschool Tutorial

Acknowledgements

Every reference book is only as strong as its fact-checkers. The following individuals were instrumental in ensuring this book presented quality, relevant information.

- Stephen Ippolito Jr. – B.A. in Elementary Education
- Second Lt. Matthew Ippolito, U.S. Army – B.A. in International Communications
- Hannah Keeler – B.A. in Cross-Cultural Studies and Biblical Languages
- Audrey Mauro – B.A. in Linguistics
- Sarah McConahy – B.A. in English Literature
- Sarah White – M.A. in TESOL and Intercultural Studies

Sincere thanks to the world's best critique partners, who were always willing to test new content and worksheets. A shout-out to Julia Busko for the awesome graphics and cover design. And an especial thanks to my husband, the biggest supporter in my teaching career, and to God, for making such an incredible world and such fascinating cultures to study.

About the Author

Janeen Ippolito is an author of creative breakthroughs in her nonfiction and speculative fiction. She writes urban fantasy, steampunk fantasy (with dragons), and paranormal romance, all featuring misfit characters in facing impossible odds. She's also an experienced entrepreneur, author coach, editor, teacher, and the president of Uncommon Universes Press. Whether brainstorming a new plot twist or analyzing new marketing angles, Janeen is happiest when creating breakthroughs for her hapless characters and for the amazing authors and businesspeople she works with in the ever-changing publishing industry.

Using her knowledge and degree in cross-cultural communication, Janeen created *World-Building From the Inside Out*, a highly-rated world building textbook and workbook that offer a culturally-conscious perspective on creating science fiction and fantasy worlds. In her spare time, Janeen can be found reading, writing, cooking, watching geeky TV shows, or sword-fighting with her husband. Two of her side goals in life are eating a fried tarantula and traveling to Antarctica.

Additional Help

Thanks for reading!
I hope you're inspired to build the best story cultures that you can!

Please leave a review online (Amazon.com, Barnes and Noble, Goodreads) giving feedback and mentioning any ways this book helped you. Reviews feed writers. Plus, I love feedback! Reader feedback led to the *World Building From the Inside Out* workbook.

For additional help, check out my website and sign up for my newsletter! **http://www.janeenippolito.com**

Get your seven steps to self-editing your manuscript here: **https://janeenippolito.com/author-services/resources/**

Join Creative Breakthroughs for Writing and Publishing Your Fiction, a Facebook group for additional author support! **https://www.facebook.com/groups/1435958919779131/**

Also, feel free to connect with me online with any further questions, or just to say hello!

Facebook: https://www.facebook.com/janeenippolitocreative
Pinterest: https://www.pinterest.com/janeen_ippolito/
Twitter: https://twitter.com/JaneenIppolito